T0209185

THE
FORMULA

TORY JACKSON

authorHOUSE®

AuthorHouse™
1663 Liberty Drive
Bloomington, IN 47403
www.authorhouse.com
Phone: 833-262-8899

Published by AuthorHouse 10/07/2020

ISBN: 978-1-6655-0314-3 (sc)
ISBN: 978-1-6655-0315-0 (e)

Library of Congress Control Number: 2020919442

Print information available on the last page.

This book is printed on acid-free paper.

Scripture quotations marked KJV are from the Holy Bible, King James
Version (Authorized Version). First published in 1611. Quoted from the KJV
Classic Reference Bible, Copyright © 1983 by The Zondervan Corporation.

Preface

As men we have to tune in to God's broadcast station. Most of us have had this station all our lives and never listened to or watched it, but this station has saved lives and families and changed men and women all over the world. And yet many people leave the area of the broadcast and never get it.

What is this station? Where can I get it? Is it free, and will it cost me anything? Yes, my friend, it has a cost; in some cases it will cost you all that you have. The cost will be great because this station has been here for years and will certainly outlive you. It's none other than the Word of God, his guide to everlasting life, his formula.

1
The Basics

There are basic things that men should have: the love for God, the heart for God, the strength of God, and the knowledge of God. Let's break it down.

The Love. The first is love because that's what God is and how he feels about everything he has made. We should love all that is good and pleasing to him and hate all that's evil and unacceptable to God.

The Heart. The center of the body is the heart. Without it people will perish: they won't be able to feel love or have compassion for anything. Without heart you will be an empty shell walking around with no peace, no mission, and no place to store any of the love God has for you.

The Strength. One must have the strength of God to stand against the trickery and cunning of the enemy. Without strength you won't be able to go through the trials that life will throw at you and still be able to stand after the battle is won. You must depend on God's power to guide your life. When God stands with you, failing is nonexistent. Nothing can defeat you.

The Knowledge. The mind of God is so vital to our lives and is so close to love that it will give us discernment and the ability to make the decisions that can help save our own lives and the lives of others. Having God's mind will allow you to counterattack the enemy when he presents himself.

These are four important elements of living. This training will guide you into becoming more Christlike, producing great things in you such as honor, integrity, and success. Having these qualities will make you valuable to the kingdom of God.

2

LOVE

Do we really understand the meaning of the word *love*? I thought I did until I submitted myself to Jesus. Men and women play on the word like a card game, and most won't take the risk unless they can see through the deck or until the card is flipped and they have the highest trump card. Now we're all in— or are we?

But until I let Jesus reveal what that word really means, I had the same look that's probably on your face right now, thinking: *I know what love is. Been loving my life, my spouse, and Jesus all my life. What's he talking about?* The truth is most of us don't get half of what it means to truly love.

God's love is unconditional. He will never leave us or forsake us. We can never be separated from his love and touch. He is all around us, and there is nothing he hasn't touched. He is there loving us when we do dirt, and he forgives us when we repent over and over again. He even gives us blessing through all our faults. He loves us so much, he gave his only Son.

Can we love like that? Are we willing to make the necessary changes and sacrifices that God requires of us? The only way to truly love is to spend time with God, learning all that he wants from us, being saved through his Son, Jesus, and becoming better men and women. When you receive God's love into your heart, you will learn how to love far beyond yourself. You will be transformed into the man God created you to be. This is something that's already inside you; all you have to do is tap into it.

Step into God's world and start spending time with him, no matter what the flesh wants. You have to recondition yourself if you want to help yourself and others. Trust God with your life.

Trusting God with your life may be something that you don't understand. Obeying and following guidelines from something we have never seen takes trust and love. It's the same feeling you have when you decide to start a relationship with someone: you don't know what's going to happen or how it will turn out, but you take a chance and dive in.

Sometimes we go knee-deep in putting our hearts on the line. We trust that the other person will take care of us, believe in us, have our best interests in mind, and be loyal to us at all times. This person will stand with us through all the tough times, never leave our side, and always have our back. This person will laugh and cry with us, comfort us, and forgive us—someone we can depend on no matter what. That sounds like a wonderful person, the kind that everyone wants by his or her side. Well, that's who God is!

God will be all those things and much more. He will play many roles in your life—a teacher, a producer, a friend—and orchestrate all things in your life. I have talked to Jesus so many times, thanking him and his Father for all that's been done for me. I want to please him so much. I want to make him smile and say that he's "well pleased" with me.

I've asked Jesus to show me how to love him more and praise him more and to help me with the things I'm doing and not doing in order to love God better. He has loved us for so long, and yet there are still people who don't know his name or how to love and depend on him to the fullest extent.

Show me how to make this come forth. Teach me how to love!

3

THE THINGS THAT GOD WILL DO

God is so awesome in how he reveals things to us. I'm going through what I call the last stage of "getting the junk out." This process may be the easiest of all the lessons life with God will bring to you—or it can be the hardest.

Accepting God into your life is the start. You may think that his ways are too hard or no fun; in other words, when you see the things that you're doing are not on his menu, you may think, *This task of getting my life in order is something I might not be able to do.*

But once you get over yourself, you will begin to see things in a different light, until you get to the point where you trust and believe in him. You will go through stages.

Stage 1: unbelief. This is the stage where you think this thing called serving God is a joke. You will see only a small part of the things he has in store for you. You will find yourself asking a lot of questions. *In order to get the most out of God, I have to do all* this? *I don't see why these things I'm doing are so bad. I'm a good person. I know who Jesus is.*

For those who have never heard of him, accepting him may be difficult. Entering into the realm of Jesus requires many things, including fear, obedience, wisdom, service, sacrifice, loyalty, honor, integrity, respect, bravery, joy, and everything else we need to compose the making of something we don't understand. But once you open up yourself to his love, you will experience something unexplainable. His love is breathtaking, something you must feel, and once you do, you will want more.

Stage 2: doubt. Following unbelief is the stage of doubt. The thoughts will turn into words: *Why me? They won't listen to me. I steal things; I sell and do drugs. I cheat my way through things; I hurt people. I drink too much. They'll laugh at me. I'll lose all my friends.*

If all these things are bad for you, God wants you to give them up anyway. I know you have created a nice comfort zone for yourself, but it's time to let it go. Living for God will require you to be flexible, firm, and strong. The enemy will try to play on all your bad attributes, telling you that this new path of life you're on is bad, weak; it will not end well; it won't make you happy or better. All these things Satan tells us are lies. He has no power, only what we give him.

That's why Jesus tells us to upgrade our armor. Ephesians 6:10–11 says:

> *Finally, be strengthened in the lord and in the strength of his power. Clothe yourselves with the full armor of God so that you may be able to stand against the schemes of the devil.*

Getting into the Word of God will help you achieve this. We men especially need to be solid in the Word of God, and we have to be solid in our lives, not just for ourselves but for our families. They depend on us to do the right thing even when we want to rebel. Men have to be leaders in our homes, work, and the church. We have to be examples to other men and show them how to be strong, righteous, and willing to stand up, be bold against darkness, and do all the things that God loves with *no* exceptions.

4

LEADERS

Men have accomplished many things in their lives, and most if not all required them to lead. Being a leader can be hard for many of us, or it can be very easy, though there is a lot of responsibility attached. You have to be strong and willing to do the work.

I didn't come into my true leadership role until I was told what responsibilities come with this lifestyle. The main thing was that I had to die to self, give things up, and trust and believe in myself. I had to realize that I couldn't do anything without God teaching me how to be an effective leader. I had to believe that I could do anything; I could not fight myself, and I had to eliminate all doubt. I knew that if I truly believed and trusted God, then as long as I had him backing me up, I would not fall.

Leading will require you to make tough decisions. Sometimes you will seem uncool, and many won't understand the way you do things, but stay on track—don't lose your focus. It's important to understand the power that comes with leadership and not to abuse it, always checking yourself and staying on point, staying grounded.

Issues will arise in our lifetime, some bigger than others, and how we choose to handle them will determine our growth, strength, and maturity. Those in turn will help us become great leaders; being deeply engaged in the ways of God will help us overcome anything.

5

A GOOD FOUNDATION

Having God in your life as your leader will create stability, give you good ground to stand on, and transform you into a strong man.

Everything is built on a foundation; nothing will stand if the foundation is faulty. The key to a strong foundation is relentless attention to detail. A foundation provides stability from the ground up to carry the weight of the structure and avoid unequal settling.

A foundation is an idea, a principle, or a fact that provides support for something or someone. This comes into play whether you are single or married and whether or not you have children. We have to be solid in our homes, being good fathers and great husbands. We need to take care of our children and wives. Women need us to be strong, protect them, love them, and grow with them, always praying for and with them.

A woman needs her man to be like a tree. Trees are strong and solid, grounded, and able to withstand mighty winds. A strong tree is not easily broken or knocked down. The roots of a tree are deep in the ground and can extend into the ground as much as twenty feet in all directions. Tree roots absorb and transfer moisture and nutrients and also provide support for the above ground portion, serving a variety of functions for the tree.

A tree's roots dig deep into the earth, and its branches reach high into the sky, accepting energy from the sun. Trees provide food and shelter and help us breathe. The branches grow in all directions and produce leaves, which provide shade for a cool place to rest. Trees come in many shapes and colors and are very beautiful, and some even have flowers.

But some men get confused, choosing to be a leaf instead of a tree. Although they come from the same root, leaves only last for a season. They will fall off and lie on the ground, fragile, doing nothing, losing their color and life, and finally being blown away by the wind or picked up and burned. And even though they will return next season, they will still end up being discarded while the tree remains standing.

God loves us so much that he gives us free will. He gives us instructions on how to live a life filled with his love and guidance. To extend the metaphor, when we start out as little trees, he will give us food (his Word), with energy from the sun (the Holy

Spirit), and supply life-giving water. All this combines together so that we may grow into healthy, strong trees.

So which are you, the strong foundation, or the leaves that get blown away season after season?

6

NEW THINGS

The time will come when we put away old things and start off fresh, when we throw away the old faded, broken, and battered pieces of our lives and start off with new things.

Everyone loves new things. They can be anything: cars, games, homes, jobs, and even relationships. The list can grow long. But sometimes things lose their luster and shine; our interest fades, and the things grow tasteless and flat. We as people will get tired of most of the things we get, learn, or see; we'll betray the very things we wanted so much.

But God will never trade us in. His love never dies, his will never fades, and his mercy, favor, and grace never expire. His strength won't get dull with age; his wisdom will only get better. His knowledge and power will only increase. He is almighty and awesome and utterly worthy of our praise. He is giving, kind, loving, and generous. He never grows tired of us, and he loves it when we seek him out and find new things in him.

When you let God inside your life, everything is new. His blessings are incredible. His Word will flow through you and change your life. You'll want to experience more of him and his glory.

So don't be afraid of trying new things. Life happens in an instant, and the changes come unexpectedly. No matter what, you have to adapt to the change. It's the same with your life: God has boundless blessings in store for you. Don't miss the opportunity to experience the new and fantastic things he has for you. Great things are about to happen for you.

7

BUILDUP

It's time for men to go through the buildup experience, where all things in God's realm are helpful to them through Christ. God is tired of men being weak and simpleminded. It's time to replace all things that are broken and faulty and downright no good so they can be destroyed in this process that God wants to put us through.

His goal is to impart the power behind this gift. A strong man is required; not everyone will pass this test because it will require you give up all things that are unacceptable to God. But if you go through this process, it will leave you stronger, wiser, and full of the Holy Spirit, and you'll have a better understanding of God. Most who start this process will drop out because it's easy to quit, and some of us believe we're already all right. But when you start this process, your prayer and thoughts and speech will all go to higher levels.

I was sitting on the bed listening to God talk, and when he told me about this, it knocked me to my knees. It all came from a letter I wrote to a friend who was in jail. I wanted to tell him something that would help him, and God gave it to me later that night: *Build up.* Everyone needs it, but men do especially, because God made us the head; we're made to lead. We have many responsibilities not only to ourselves but to our families. We have to be the light in dark places, destroying evil at the moment it shows up.

The process is amazing and very simple. You may

be saying, "What if I fail? Do I only get one shot with Jesus?" Of course not. God will never leave us; we're the ones who leave him. To achieve buildup, we simply need to seek and accept all the bad things in our lives. Once that's done, we need to go to God in prayer, tell him all the dirt that's in us, and ask him to take it away.

Go through each negative trait and habit and all that makes you bad and ashamed and ask God to take it away, but as you ask him to take away something bad, ask him to replace it with something good.

Go to him with an honest and willing heart, and believe that he can heal all the wounds and hurt and guilt in your life. And don't leave anything out. I understand that some of us have things inside that we don't want anyone to know about, but the beauty of it all is that God already knows what's there. So speak up, ask him to take it away and replace it with his blessings, and he will pour his Holy Spirit on you.

Go to him with all the things *you know* are inside you, but also ask him to show you the things inside you that *you don't know*. That's the real start of buildup. Exposing yourself will open you up so that God can come in and change your way of thinking. Your prayer will change, and your whole outlook will also.

Ephesians 6:10–18 talks about putting on the whole armor of God so you can be able to stand against the schemes of the devil. We have to stay seeking God at all times because the devil never stops; he is on the prowl always. You are special to God, and he loves you unconditionally. He gave his only Son to die for your sins.

He wants you to win and to live an abounded life full of love and joy. So go full speed ahead, and discover all that God has for you. *You will not lose!*

8

TIME WITH GOD

We have to learn to spend as much time in the Word of God as possible. We often pile all our issues into our heads, and most of the time we don't know how to deal with them. At one point in my life I had endless issues going on, and I didn't know how to deal with them correctly. I thought I was solving them, but they kept coming back.

My knowledge was limited, and I was working them out the best I could, but they kept growing until it felt like they were as big as a planet. Now you might say that's a little extreme, but that's how I felt.

I was trying to balance countless things at once, and every day another problem seemed to be waiting.

There was one serious problem that I thought I had a handle on, but it kept getting bigger and bigger. I thought that "out of sight, out of mind" was fixing it. But not dealing with it head on and getting help only made it worse. Finally, when it blew up in my face and spilled all over my family, I admitted to myself that I couldn't fix it on my own. I went to my pastor, discussed it with him, and asked what to do. He told me to go into the closet and spend time with God.

I was scared at first, but if I wanted to get help—and I definitely needed healing—I had to go in there. What could it harm? I was already dealing with the pain of hurting my family and letting myself down for not dealing with it sooner. This was the only way to fix it. I had just given my life over to Jesus, and I wanted to know everything about him and how to change my lifestyle from the way I had been living it. My wife and I had a new son, and I needed to be a better man, husband, and father, so I had to do it.

The first night I went in, God said, "What are you doing in here?"

I said, "I want to talk to you."

He said, "Sit down and shut up." I did just that and sat silently for eight hours. Then he said, "Get up and go to bed."

The next night I was back. He said, "So you're back again?" I said yes, and he said, "Sit down and shut up." I sat there for six hours with nothing but silence. Then he said, "Get up and go to bed."

The next night, when I went back, he said, "So you're back again? Do you know why I told you the last two nights to sit down and shut up in silence for all those hours?" I said no. He said, "I wanted to know whether you were interested in me and whether you would wait. Now we can talk."

The next months were filled with knowledge and wisdom as God just talked to me about all sorts of things. I was finding out things about myself and about him: what he wants for me, and how he never left me, and how much he loves me. We addressed all my issues and concerns, and he helped me solve them all. He instilled wisdom and knowledge and understanding and taught me how to be a better man, for myself and my family.

God loves us more than we can ever fathom, and he will be there for us no matter what. He's given us much more than we deserve. We spend so much time doing useless things, pouring our time and energy into whatever we want to do. Meanwhile, there is a *lot* of God to experience. His love is awesome, his power is unmatched, his wisdom is outstanding, and there is nothing that he hasn't touched. He's in everything, on earth and beyond, which makes him infinite.

Spending time with God will also open new avenues you haven't explored and give you insight into your gifts and talents. There is a great deal laid up inside of us, and most of us have no idea what hidden abilities we have. God will unlock us to be at our full potential and make us whole; all we have to do is let him.

The way through this process is called dying to self. Dying to self is when we fully submit to God, get out of our own way, and let all useless things go. No matter how much we want to control what's going on in our lives, if what we're doing isn't helping us and serves no purpose, why are we holding on to it? If we still have the same problems and haven't found solutions, we should let them go and give them to God to handle. This is the essence of dying to self: letting a different, much better way into our lives, releasing and handing over total control, and accepting a change into our hearts.

The process can be hard or go easy, depending on how soon and how badly you need it in your life. Regardless, it will only help and not hurt you. God can and will do wonderful things in your life; just open up and receive all that he has for you. The devil will tell you that changing is a waste of time, that God won't do anything for you, that you're fine the way you are, and that if you decide to follow God, nothing good will come of it. He insists that serving God will cost you everything you've built for yourself; people will look at you funny, and you'll lose all your friends and family. The devil will probably say all this and more, but the truth is that he will always try to tear you down whether you serve God or not. The devil simply doesn't want you to win at all.

Yes, it's true that changing your life will cost you something, but Jesus loves you so much that he will restore all that's lost. Let me tell you something that happened to me. I gave my life to Jesus in 2008. Before that I was raised a Jehovah's witness. By the time I was sixteen, I was questioning whether that was right for me, due to something that had happened. I stole some money, and my mom turned me in to the elders of the congregation. They sat me down and questioned me about what I'd done. Then they told me to step out while they consulted God because I couldn't. After a few minutes they called me back in and told me that I was to be kicked out and that I couldn't talk or associate with anybody from the congregation. I was disfellowshipped until God told them (not me) that I could return to the flock. God had turned his back on me, and so did everyone else.

I was driving home with my mom, and the whole

time I kept thinking about what the Bible said, that I could go to God and ask for forgiveness of my sins. If that was true, why had I sat before three men who said I wasn't qualified to do so? When I asked my mom this question, she went off, saying not to question the elders, because they knew best.

I know that story is a bit of a tangent, but it all leads back to 2008. I gave my life to Jesus, and I was learning about God in a different light. He doesn't throw us away or leave us. My pastor, James C. Tibbs, was teaching me all sorts of things about Jesus, and I was soaking it all in.

I was having trouble reading the Bible; I just couldn't find the time. My friend Gerald told me to put the Bible by the front door where my keys were and give myself enough time before I went to work to read one chapter a day, and I would advance more as time went on. After finishing the first chapter I heard in my head, *You're gonna lose your job today*. I dismissed it and went on to work, but just as sure as I'd heard, I lost my job for not taking a lunch break!

At the time this happened I had a four-bedroom house and a minivan and a nice amount of money in the bank. In the next six months, I lost it all. I had to move into a two-bedroom apartment with my brother and his wife and their five kids. I had three kids, and my wife was pregnant with our fourth.

This is where the story gets crazy, God told me not to work for two years, and in that time I was to get to know him and trust him. He said that he would take care of all my needs. In that time the only job I was able to get was food delivery. All was lost but the minivan, which was gone a year later. People couldn't understand it when I told them what God had told me. My wife's brother told me one day that he saw the changes God was doing in my life, but since I had started serving God, I had lost everything, and if I lost everything by doing this, then it was out of the question for him to do it.

Those two years changed our lives. I learned so much and fixed many issues in my life. I won't tell you that it was all good all the time; a lot of my problems caused me emotional and embarrassing turmoil in my family. But God said in all things, count it all as joy. No matter how bad it gets or how low we may fall, God is there. He will help us, save us from the hands of the devil, and even save us from ourselves. God wants us to trust him through anything; there's nothing beyond his reach.

It was always easy for me to trust him once I experienced him for the first time at the age of sixteen. I trust him with everything, and I won't ever turn back. After we went through all that in the course of about two and half years, God restored everything:

the house, three cars, and a new business to bring in a hefty income.

God will restore your life in abundant blessings. Living for Jesus will cause you to have everlasting life. Life will throw you all kinds of trouble and challenges; some will cut you really deep, and you may find yourself questioning your faith, wondering why this is happening to you or why that is happening in the world. I can tell you from personal experience that if you want answers, just call on Jesus. He will never let you down.

So no matter what, keep praying and living a righteous life, and when you fall, shake it off, get back up, and ask God to give you strength, wisdom, and peace to get through it and keep going. Understand that there's a lesson in everything. Remember that Jesus is there when things are great, and he is there when the pain comes. Just remember to praise him through it all, good and bad.

9

FINAL THOUGHTS

I pray that this has helped you and that it will get you on track to either seek God or to dig deeper into God. Jesus only wants the best for you. Everything that I am and have is because of Jesus; without him I am nothing. I can't make it without him.

Am I perfect? Not at all. Do I fall? Oh yeah! A day in the life of Tory Jackson is a crazy one, but I can't get through that day without Jesus. I love my life, and I live my life as righteously as I can. God hasn't failed me and never will. I trust him with my heart, and I share my experience and knowledge of him with my family and anyone else I can.

So keep praying, and let integrity and uprightness preserve you. Stay in the game; be a player and an onlooker, never slacking, even when you get tired and want to give up. Ask Jesus to place the Holy Spirit and mercy on you. Stay in God's Word; learn it, live it, and give it to others. Stay focused, stay on course, and stay grounded.

Remember that transformation is the key, and it happens on the inside. You have to submit and renew your mind to grow in Jesus. Transformation will take you to a higher place in God where all things in your life are better.

Always be true to yourself. You can't be transformed if you lie to yourself. Be direct; God is that way, so give yourself the same treatment. A spiritual mind is able to be activated by the truth factor. And don't be carnal minded; it will produce manipulation and self-justification. These are things you don't need in your life.

Be open to the changes God wants to make in your life. God will only pour into vessels that are without lids. This occurs when you submit to him, so be humble, and don't fight. He wants to do this for you. Submit to God. Then he can lead you to do great things.

Be flexible. You have to open up to constant movement. God is always moving, changing things in his path to make them better. Trust the Lord, and again, be open. Exposure to God is a good thing. He will be able to cleanse you with his love.

There's a great deal to experience in the Lord, endless joy and an abundant life. So pray and listen, and ask the Holy Spirit to reveal Jesus to you. Salvation awaits, blindness will be gone, and you will take new territory. Jesus will reshape your clay, and you will go to another level. Great leaders are changed when they open themselves up to God.

There is order in everything, so structure yourself to be the best. I believe in you. I wish you peace and blessings, and may your life be complete.

Printed in the United States
By Bookmasters